christmas
wishes

christmas
wishes

inspiring lessons for the festive season

www.youaretheauthor.com

Published in the UK in 2003 exclusively for
WHSmith Limited
Greenbridge Road
Swindon SN3 3LD
www.WHSmith.co.uk
by Tangent Publications, an imprint of
Axis Publishing Limited.

Conceived and created by
Axis Publishing Limited
8c Accommodation Road
London NW11 8ED
www.axispublishing.co.uk

Creative Director: Siân Keogh
Managing Editor: Brian Burns
Production Manager: Tim Clarke

ISBN 0–9543620–8–X

2 4 6 8 10 9 7 5 3 1

Printed and bound in China

www.youaretheauthor.com

about this book

Christmas Wishes brings together an inspirational selection of powerful and life-affirming phrases that in one way or another have touched people's lives during the festive season, and combines them with evocative and gently amusing animal photographs that bring out the full humour and pathos of the human condition.

Christmas is a time of joy and thanks giving, but it's all too easy to lose sight of this in the midst of all the preparations, parties and presents. These inspiring examples of wit and wisdom, written by real people based on their real-life experiences, enable us to regain our sense of perspective and rediscover the true meaning of Christmas. As one of the entries so aptly puts it – it's the warmth that comes to our hearts when the Christmas spirit returns again.

So here's to a happy Christmas and a healthy, prosperous and peaceful New Year.

about the author

Why have one author when you can have the world? This book has been compiled using the incredible resource that is the world wide web. From the many hundreds of contributions that were sent to the website, *www.youaretheauthor.com*, we have selected the ones that best sum up what Christmas is all about – peace on earth, good will to all men, and a stocking full of presents!

Please continue to send in your special views, feelings and advice about life – you never know, you too might see your wise words in print one day!

www.youaretheauthor.com

The perfect Christmas is a frozen land full of warmth.

There's nothing better than snowfall outside, a good fire inside and good cheer and amiable company all around.

anon@youaretheauthor.com

May your days be merry and your heart be light, your holidays happy and your season bright.

saramatthews12@hotmail.com

May Christmas bring
friends to your side
and happiness to your
New Year.

Never choose to be alone at this
time of year – it's all about
reawakening your spirit for
the year to come.

greg_green_2@yahoo.co.uk

Friends make
Christmas merry!

And a nice warm drop makes
it even merrier!

abi37@hotmail.com

Your friendship is the nicest
Christmas gift of all.

I always make sure to see
everyone I know in the run-up to
Christmas, especially if I haven't
seen them for a while.

anon@youaretheauthor.com

Though miles
apart, you're
in our hearts
at Christmas!

So remember to phone!

suphetty76@hotmail.com

Christmas is a time when you get homesick – even when you're home.

anon@youaretheauthor.com

Christmas is the only time that we sit around looking at a dead tree and eating chocolate out of our socks!

anon@youaretheauthor.com

Relax now, the bird
is in the oven.

Eventually, the preparation ends
and the feasting begins.

anon@youaretheauthor.com

Christmas is not a
time or a season,
but a state of mind.

I can even think my way into
a Christmas mood at any time
of the year and it always helps
to cheer me up.

stephanie_frances@yahoo.co.uk

Until you feel the spirit of Christmas, there is no Christmas.

That's why I like to start feeling it
around about mid-November.

brandon_top@musician.org

There is no ideal Christmas;
only the Christmas you decide
to make as a reflection
of your values, desires,
affections and traditions.

Geoffrey_Howarth@hotmail.com

There has been only one Christmas – the rest are anniversaries.

But that's OK by me because you can never have too many anniversaries.

greg_green_2@yahoo.co.uk

Christmas began in the heart of God.

It is complete only when it reaches the heart of man.

Even if it's only for five minutes, put a little time aside to remember what it's all about.

anon@youaretheauthor.com

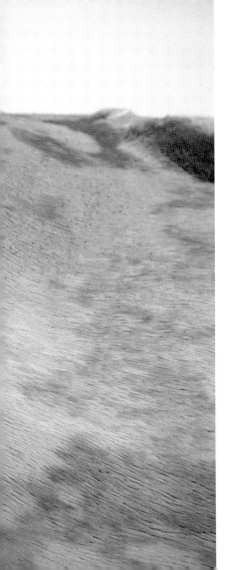

It's the warmth
that comes to our
hearts when the
Christmas spirit
returns again.

melanie_williams_2@hotmail.com

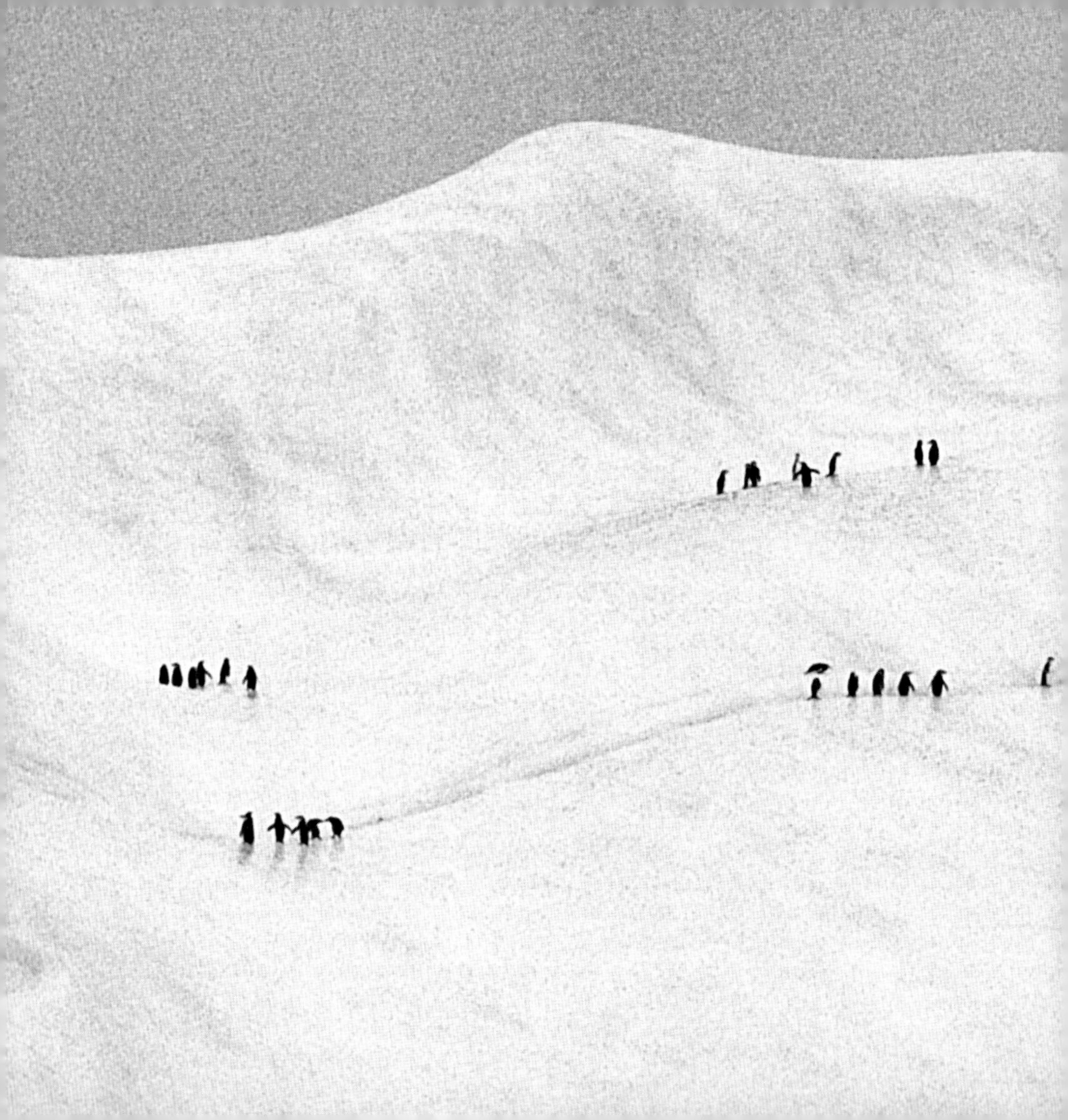

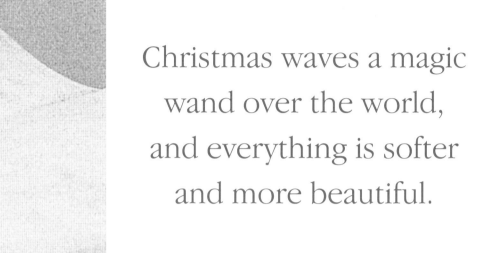

Christmas waves a magic
wand over the world,
and everything is softer
and more beautiful.

None of us should ever forget
that we need to hold on to some
magic in our lives.

anon@youaretheauthor.com

Perhaps the best Yuletide decoration is being wreathed in smiles.

Think about it – during the festive
season, you smile at complete
strangers in a way that you never
normally do, and it makes you feel
so good. Why don't you do it
more often?

Thomas_Elliot@hotmail.com

All I want for
Christmas is my
two front teeth.

anon@youaretheauthor.com

The sparkle in a
child's eyes shines
brighter than any
Christmas lights.

It is true that Christmas is really
for kids, but that doesn't mean
you can't be a kid for a day.

saramatthews12@hotmail.com

Don't worry about
the size of your
Christmas tree.

In the eyes of children,
they are all 30 feet tall.

anon@youaretheauthor.com

Christmas, children, is not a date.
It is a state of mind.

anon@youaretheauthor.com

There's nothing sadder in this world than to awake on Christmas morning and not be a child.

So go on – be one!

Geoffrey_Howarth@hotmail.com

The magic of
Christmas is that
we all become
children again.

Christmas is for
children of all ages.

rog2llus@yahoo.com

This Christmas, with
quietness of mind;
let us always be patient
and kind.

I find it's a good time of year to
forgive and forget, put things
behind me and start afresh.

anon@youaretheauthor.com

Put your shoes by your
bed on Christmas Eve
to prevent the
family quarreling.

melanie_williams_2@hotmail.com

On Christmas Eve all animals can speak. However, it is bad luck to test this superstition.

anon@youaretheauthor.com

Good luck will come to
the home where a fire is
kept burning throughout
the Christmas season.

And I shouldn't have to tell
you that the fire burns brightest
in your heart.

melanie_williams_2@hotmail.com

What I don't like about office Christmas parties is looking for a job the next day.

anon@youaretheauthor.com

Why is Christmas just like
a day at the office ?

You do all the work and
the fat guy with the suit
gets all the credit.

saffyshar@hotmail.com

There was a time when
I was younger that I didn't
believe in Santa Claus…

Now I know that
Santa Claus exists.

anon@youaretheauthor.com

When you stop believing in Santa Claus you get underwear for Christmas.

mark.sit@lycos.com

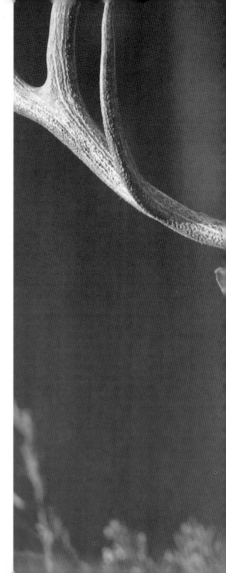

You know you're getting old, when Santa starts looking younger.

Then again, when you've reached that age, you can do a lot worse than fat and jolly...

brandon_top@musician.org

Be naughty – save
Santa a trip!

mariollah@yahoo.com

What do you call
people who are afraid of
Santa Claus?

Claustrophobic.

All together now...
quack, quack!

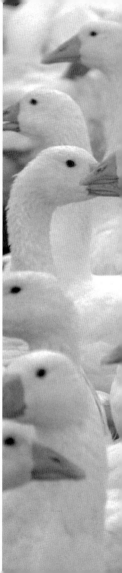

abi37@hotmail.com

Why does Scrooge love Rudolph
the Red-Nosed Reindeer?

Because every buck is
dear to him.

Christmas is a time when kids tell Santa what they want and their parents pay for it.

Much like the rest of the year,
except for the Santa bit.

greg_green_2@yahoo.co.uk

I bought my kids a set of
batteries for Christmas…

with a note on them saying,
toys not included.

anon@youaretheauthor.com

Give books for Christmas. They're never fattening, seldom sinful, and permanently personal.

Make reading a delight for children at Christmas and it will be a habit for life.

suphetty76@hotmail.com

Christmas is a time when everybody wants his past forgotten and his present remembered.

There is always
somebody that one
is afraid not to
give a Christmas
present to.

Blessed are those who can give without remembering, and take without forgetting.

As a child, I'll be honest, I never could understand the idea that it was better to give than to receive. But to understand this – truly in your heart – means you've come a long way in life.

mike_pritch20@yahoo.com

You might as well
do your Christmas
hinting early.

anon@youaretheauthor.com

Even before Christmas has said 'Hello', it's saying 'Buy Buy'.

melanie_williams_2@hotmail.com

Christmas is a race to see
which gives out first –
your money or your feet.

anon@youaretheauthor.com

A Christmas shopper's complaint is one of long-standing.

Ask yourself – unless it's likely to break a child's heart, break off an engagement, or break up a marriage, is it really worth it?

Geoffrey_Howarth@hotmail.com

Many banks have a new
kind of Christmas club
in operation.

It helps you save money
to pay for last year's gifts.

Bah… humbug!

If there is no joyous way to give a festive gift, give love away.

It's the one sure way it will bounce back.

stephanie_frances@yahoo.co.uk

Remember,
love weighs more
than gold.

anon@youaretheauthor.com

It is love in the heart that puts Christmas in the air.

Love is what you hear on Christmas morning, when you stop opening presents and listen.

It is the sound of a child running around the room, squealing with delight.

Thomas_Elliot@hotmail.com

You don't need Christmas
in your hands…

when you have Christmas
in your heart.

anon@youaretheauthor.com

If you don't have Christmas in your heart, you will never find it under a tree.

And nor, for that matter, can you leave it under the tree for anyone else to find.

abi37@hotmail.com

To cherish peace and goodwill is to have the real spirit of Christmas.

anon@youaretheauthor.com

Next to a circus
there ain't nothing
that packs up
and tears out
faster than the
Christmas spirit.

anon@youaretheauthor.com

If only we could put Christmas spirit in jars and open a jar of it every month.

saramatthews12@hotmail.com

I will honour Christmas in
my heart, and try to keep
it all the year.

Of course this isn't easy – but
truly good things are rarely easy.

anon@youaretheauthor.com

Christmas ain't over 'til the fat angel sings!

So join in – for there is nothing
like a Christmas song to clear
your head, warm your heart
and lift your spirit.

May Peace be your gift at
Christmas and your blessing
all year through!

anon@youaretheauthor.com